W9-AVY-753

Disgusting Plants

BY CONNIE COLWELL MILLER

Consultant:
Jeffrey Gillman
Associate Professor
Horticultural Science
University of Minnesota

Capstone
press

Mankato, Minnesota

Blazers is published by Capstone Press,
151 Good Counsel Drive, P.O. Box 669, Mankato, Minnesota 56002.
www.capstonepress.com

Library of Congress Cataloging-in-Publication Data
Miller, Connie Colwell, 1976–
    Disgusting plants / by Connie Colwell Miller.
    p. cm.—(Blazers. That's disgusting!)
    Includes bibliographical references and index.
    ISBN-13: 978-0-7368-6802-0 (hardcover)
    ISBN-10: 0-7368-6802-X (hardcover)
    ISBN-13: 978-0-7368-7880-7 (pbk. softcover)
    ISBN-10: 0-7368-7880-7 (pbk. softcover)
    1. Plants—Miscellanea—Juvenile literature. I. Title. II. Series.
QK49.M56 2007
580—dc22   2006026493

Summary: Describes 10 disgusting plants and what makes them gross.

Editorial Credits
Mandy Robbins, editor; Thomas Emery, designer; Bob Lentz, illustrator;
    Jo Miller, photo researcher/photo editor

Photo Credits
Bill Johnson, 4–5, 13 (inset), 28–29
Bruce Coleman Inc./Ed Degginger, 10–11; Kim Taylor, 17 (inset)
Corbis/ Neil Miller; Papilio, 22–23; Reuters, 27; zefa/Theowulf Maehl, 17
Dwight R. Kuhn, 18–19
McDonald Wildlife Photography/Joe McDonald, cover
Nature Picture Library/John Waters, 7
Photo Researchers, Inc/Adam Jones, 9; Gail Jankus, 24–25
Shutterstock/Martin Bowker, 13
SuperStock/age fotostock, 14–15, 21 (poison ivy)
Visuals Unlimited/Dr. Ken Greer, 20–21 (arms with rash)

1 2 3 4 5 6 12 11 10 09 08 07

Table of Contents

That's Disgusting!

Sticky, milky goo oozes out of the milkweed plant.

People and animals can be pretty disgusting. But there are some nasty plants too. Plants often do gross things to help them grow and survive.

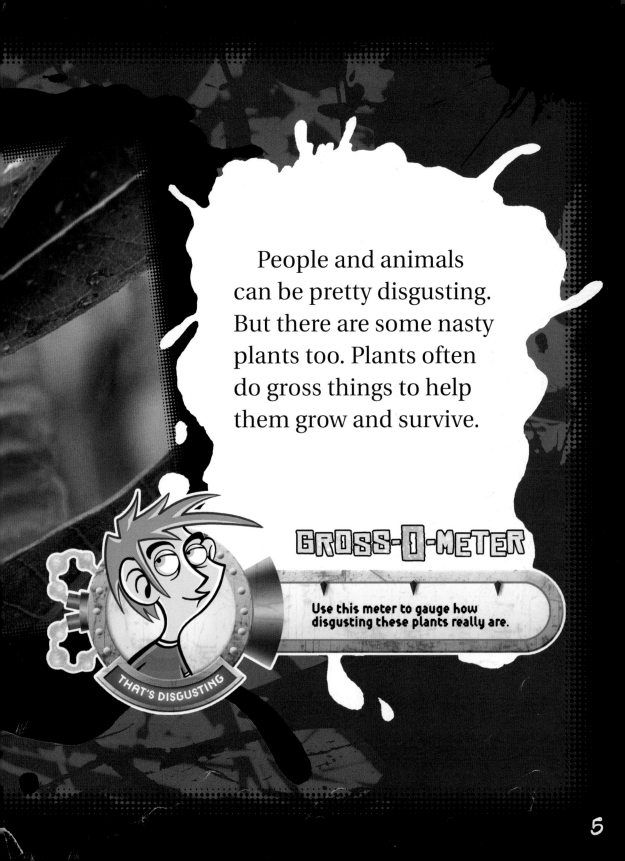

GROSS-O-METER

Use this meter to gauge how disgusting these plants really are.

THAT'S DISGUSTING

Choking Hazard

Strangler fig trees grow on the trunks of other trees. Eventually, the first tree chokes to death and rots away.

GROSS-O-METER

SORT OF DISGUSTING

Murder in the Forest

Black walnut trees kill their neighbors. Their roots poison other trees. Then the black walnut can grow bigger and stronger.

GROSS-O-METER

SORT OF DISGUSTING

9

Slip and Slide

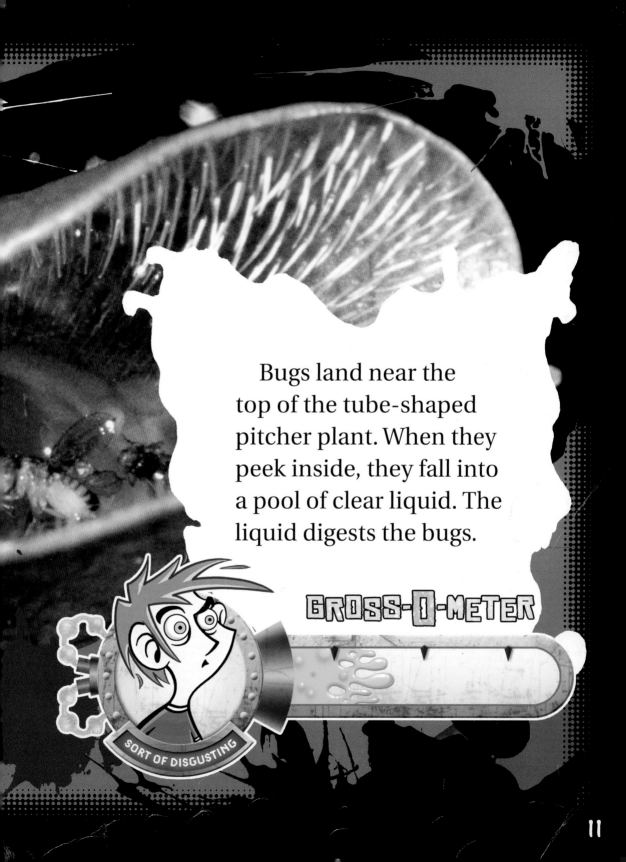

Bugs land near the top of the tube-shaped pitcher plant. When they peek inside, they fall into a pool of clear liquid. The liquid digests the bugs.

GROSS-O-METER

SORT OF DISGUSTING

What a Stink!

Stinkweed often grows in cow pastures. It gives off an awful smell. Milk from cows that have eaten stinkweed tastes bitter.

GROSS-O-METER

SORT OF DISGUSTING

Stinkweed

Fungi Food

GROSS-O-METER

PRETTY DISGUSTING

Lots of people eat mushrooms. But do you know what mushrooms eat? They feed on rotting plants and animals!

BLAZER FACT

Some mushrooms are poisonous to people and animals.

Broke the Mold

If you don't eat your fruits and vegetables, mold will. When food sits too long, a fuzzy carpet of fungus will grow on it.

GROSS-O-METER

PRETTY DISGUSTING

Moldy tomato

Bug Juice

GROSS-O-METER

PRETTY DISGUSTING

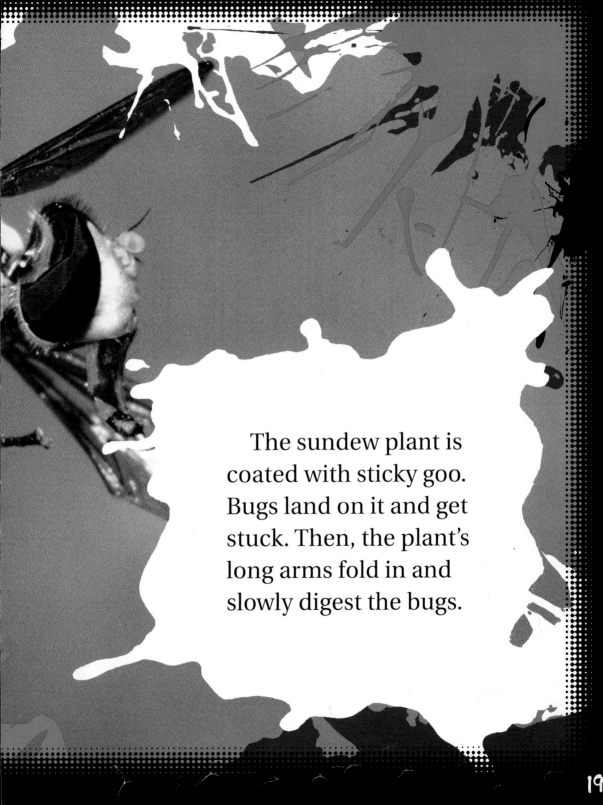

The sundew plant is coated with sticky goo. Bugs land on it and get stuck. Then, the plant's long arms fold in and slowly digest the bugs.

Itchy Plant

Touching poison ivy can cause an itchy rash on your skin. Many people also get painful pus-filled blisters.

GROSS-O-METER

PRETTY DISGUSTING

People can get a rash just by touching something that has touched poison ivy!

Bug Trap

The Venus flytrap gobbles up its food. Bugs smell the sweet plant and land on it. In an instant, the flytrap snaps its leaves shut. Yum!

GROSS-O-METER

REALLY DISGUSTING

Poisonous Parsley

Poison hemlock is a pretty plant with ugly effects. Eating just a small amount can paralyze your muscles and even cause death.

GROSS-O-METER

REALLY DISGUSTING

People have eaten
poison hemlock
thinking it was parsley.

Nature's Stink Bomb

The titan arum gives off a terrible stink when it blooms. Its enormous blossom smells like rotten meat.

GROSS-O-METER

REALLY DISGUSTING

The smell of the titan arum attracts bugs that spread the flower's seeds.

Gross and Green

The pencil cactus oozes a sticky sap that can cause blisters, burning, and even blindness.

Plants may ooze sticky goo, eat bugs, or smell awful. But these disgusting features help them survive.

We made it through, and I have one thing to say. **That's disgusting!**

Glossary

blister (BLISS-tur)—a sore bubble of skin filled with liquid such as water, pus, or blood; blisters often are caused by something rubbing against the skin.

digest (dye-JEST)—to break down food

fungus (FUHN-jye)—a type of organism that has no leaves, flowers, or roots; mushrooms and mold are fungi.

paralyze (PAR-uh-lize)—to cause a loss of the ability to control the muscles

pasture (PASS-chur)—an open field, usually fenced, where animals eat grass

poison (POI-zuhn)—a substance that can kill or harm someone; also, the act of giving someone poison.

rash (RASH)—spots or red patches on the skin that can sometimes be caused by plants

Read More

Bathroom Readers' Institute. *Uncle John's Electrifying Bathroom Reader for Kids Only.* Ashland, Ore.: Bathroom Readers' Press, 2003.

Masoff, Joy. *Oh, Yuck! The Encyclopedia of Everything Nasty.* New York: Workman, 2000.

Szpirglas, Jeff. *Gross Universe: Your Guide to All Disgusting Things Under the Sun.* Toronto, Ontario: Maple Tree Press, 2004.

Internet Sites

FactHound offers a safe, fun way to find Internet sites related to this book. All of the sites on FactHound have been researched by our staff.

Here's how:

1. Visit *www.facthound.com*

2. Choose your grade level.

3. Type in this book ID **073686802X** for age-appropriate sites. You may also browse subjects by clicking on letters, or by clicking on pictures and words.

4. Click on the **Fetch It** button.

FactHound will fetch the best sites for you!

Index